P9-EDF-171

New Shoes

ALSO BY KATHLEEN FRASER

What I Want
Stilts, Somersaults, & Headstands
(children's poems and chants)
In Limited Editions:
    Special Handling (with Laura Wessner)
    Magritte Series
    Little Notes to You, from Lucas Street
    In Defiance of the Rains
    Change of Address

New
Shoes

Kathleen Fraser

HARPER & ROW, PUBLISHERS

New York, Hagerstown, San Francisco, London

Grateful acknowledgment is made to the following publishers for permission to reprint from their limited editions of Kathleen Fraser's previous books: Tuumba Press for *Magritte Series*, © 1977 by Kathleen Fraser. Pancake Press for poems from *Special Handling* (a poem correspondence with Laura Wessner), including the poems "New Shoes," "Special Handling," " 'The Know,' " "Flood," "The Recognition" and "Dear Laura, in December," © 1978 by Kathleen Fraser.

Some of the poems in this volume have appeared in *Anteus, Aspen Anthology, Birthstone, Black Box #11, California State Poetry Quarterly, Foothill Quarterly, Hard-Pressed, Harvard Magazine, Ironwood, Mademoiselle, Out There, Seneca Review, Stooge, Trellis, ZZZZ* and in the following anthologies: *The American Poetry Anthology*, 1975, edited by Daniel Halpern, published by Avon (Equinox Books); *California Poets Bi-Centennial Anthology*, 1976, edited by A. D. Winans, published by Second Coming Press; *Contemporary Women Poets*, 1977, edited by Jennifer McDowell and M. Loventhal, Merlin Press; and *This Is Women's Work*, 1974, edited by Susan Efros, published by Panjandrum Press.

FIRST EDITION

Designed by Stephanie Krasnow

Library of Congress Cataloging in Publication Data
Fraser, Kathleen.
  New shoes.
  Poems.
  I. Title.
PS3556.R353N4 1978   811'.5'4   77-15899
ISBN 0-06-011374-X
ISBN 0-06-011380-4 pbk.

78 79 80 81 82 10 9 8 7 6 5 4 3 2 1

for my friend Art,

who taught me how to balance without a net

CONTENTS

Part I

COINCIDENTAL

Nuts and Bolts Poem for Mr. Mac Adams, Sr.   3
One of the Chapters   5
The Stranger   7
What You Need   9
The Fault   11
Hit-and-run   12
Coincidental   14
New Shoes   16

Part II

WITHOUT VOICE, WHAT SHE WITNESSED

Flowers   21
Something Keeps Glistening   22
In the Dark, a Chameleon   23
Without Voice, What She Witnessed   25
Notes to Lyn, Shimmin Ridge, Two Years Later   26
4 A.M.   30
Special Handling   31
"The Know"   33
Flood   35

Part III

THE STORY OF EMMA SLIDE   41

Part IV

MAGRITTE SERIES

La Vie Secrète IV / The Secret Life   56
L'Assassin Menace / The Assassin Menaces   57
La Baigneuse du Clair au Sombre / Bather Between
    Light and Darkness   59
L'Invention Collective / Collective Invention   61
Les Valeurs Personnelles / Personal Values   63
Les Jours Gigantesques / The Titanic Days   65
La Reproduction Interdite / Not to Be Reproduced   67
L'Éloge de la Dialectique / In Praise of Dialectic   69
La Révolution / The Revolution   72

Part V

NOW THAT THE SUBJUNCTIVE IS DYING

On This Day Awakened   77
Locations   79
The Recognition   83
The Journey   85
Dear Laura, in December   87

As in, a Man After My Own Heart   90

Gabionade   92

Because You Aren't Here to Be What I Can't Think of   96

Now That the Subjunctive Is Dying   99

"They could tell me how to paint their landscape but they couldn't tell me how to paint mine."

Georgia O'Keeffe

Part I

Coincidental

NUTS AND BOLTS POEM
FOR MR. MAC ADAMS, SR.

May I put my head on your shoulder, Mr. Mac Adams, Sr.?
My future takes on bubbles and substance
like a new sourdough formula and I know I can sell it
and convince them on the continent to take a bite,
with you as my lap, my Platonic cigar,
but more whiff to it, more longevity in the face
of disbelief, unlike the ideal, and thus
the kind of thing I can trust.

Where *do* you get your information
about Oswald's letter of tender regard? How is it, living
in Dallas, you have found the key to this century's thickness
in the *L.A. Times?*

      Drinking French wine in L'Etoile, the shadow of
the Orient whisking by in his white cotton jacket, I notice
your wife is radiant and exquisitely intact. Her face
reveals a preference for the emotional.

          You wave to her like two flags
a swimmer carries in his teeth, making signals, trying
to remember what the codebook said before the boat collapsed;
                he wants to say "Help!"
but he gets the syntax of red and blue confused
and it comes out "nuts and bolts."
          Now it's coming out from *your* mouth,
             you are the carrier of the code,
               it presents itself
in a white balloon above the table at L'Etoile,

above your son's devotion,
above your wife's gold belt shining,
next to me, discovering the thread
of the nut and bolt with its solid visual bite,
how much I need this silvery connection,
how much I want to sit on your lap and be small again,

to tell you about my father who held me,
whose study had a wooden desk with drawers full of
colored chalks, T-squares, compasses
and little metal pencils with pieces of lead held intact
by tiny nuts and bolts, which he'd show me how to use,
sitting on his lap, my head against his shoulder,
                              connecting the points
at the edge of the circle with arc after arc of fuchsia
and gold and fishy green pastels that crumbled and came off
                              in my fingers.

This is sentimental material, Mr. Mac Adams, Sr.,
and when my father got hit, head-on, he was just gone.
All his perfect body.
And when he never came back, we had to lock up.
                              But here you are, ready
for a second round, with your Texas-size cigar
                    and your sourdough formula
about to launch a revolution in the dining rooms of Europe,
                              and your belief
in the day after next.

ONE OF THE CHAPTERS

How could you be by halves,
behooved and beholden?

Held   but, oh, I wanted to be held

and want to fall
through the net's tiny squares like sunlight through cheesecloth.

What was expected of me
                                    and did I want my urge?
And certainly I recognized marriage and children.

I recognized coils and nets
and didn't think you could be double in Iowa.

But by then and for keeps I was keeping.
Seeping into the necessity
of contradiction.

But let's stop
to fill in the special quality of isolation—
a men's university town,
women cutting parsley and watching the green.

I still remember how it seemed a life.
                                    I came away laughing.
Somehow I absorbed the air itself, out of the air,
because I don't remember anyone
telling me,
            so that women have trouble with poetry
except for Emily.

Do you think I can have suffered? Do relationships keep?

I had to buy health. I gave up other options. But it was temporary.

This loose voice, no less, is crucial.
Other places pinch, but not really
to act on music suffered in the brain.

Everyone's childhood is several years later and less physical,
while the lover who promises parts of his body   lies in his body
sharing his cravings, wanting to, and can't

except in each construction
with somebody.   Some   body.

Questioning the tools. Looking at Picasso.   With you.
But isn't autobiography on the alert for bread?
It must be sniffing.

We realize how much we need, exactly. And personally,
as in a London bookstall, wondering if I could afford to buy,
with the heart of Sara Crewe in my heart   the same heart
and her penny for a hot bun
as her velvet dress becomes smaller and smaller and her father
forgets her.

Note: This poem includes and responds to phrases from Jane Cooper's essay, "Nothing has been used in the manufacture of this poetry that could have been used in the manufacture of bread" (*Maps & Windows*, Macmillan, 1974).

THE STRANGER

"It is yourself you fall in love with" when the mysterious stranger
appears with his solution of soft drinks.

You like to think about Pepsi and RC Cola and those sweaty
Dr. Peppers in the lower grades
                and the green play yards not yet all asphalt.
And then He comes.
Like a jungle jim of peculiar but apprehensive right angles
and you know in your heart you can climb him.

It is the shining and the light you can see flowing amidst the cubes
and he is your *self*
                or that steely part of you that seeks definition
and wants to sturdy yourself
as an alloy of metals creates an argument of strength.

The little girl games you loved,
the giant popcorn in cardboard cartons greasy with fake butter,
the bigger-than-life bodies that awaited your feelings' membrane—
all tell you
                you must set aside the metallic thrust of sadness.
It is a kind of sobbing that gets started and doesn't want to stop.
You would wish to curl up inside its waters,
float through moist black-and-white romances
and have your solitude in luxurious technicolor,
thinking you are moving,
                     while from out here we can see
that you may be stuck
in the compromise of whole-heartedness,

when on the other side of this childhood a flag is waiting,
with its code
locked into two existing colors and the key is in your feelings
which are about to bear fruit in those clear reds and yellows.

Note: This poem includes and responds to phrases from Jane Cooper's essay, "Nothing has been used in the manufacture of this poetry that could have been used in the manufacture of bread" (*Maps & Windows*, Macmillan, 1974).

WHAT YOU NEED

What you need is
a compliment to plump you up

tired ass down flat to blue chair
                          (supposed to be a touch of brightness)
yes
your mind jumped at *that* when she said how are you
and you tried not to tell

but to be a sample and a dimple
and finding the proper response to goodness,
                          to a really kind question.

And then he handed it to you,
the quick observation that you looked beautiful and oh
your heart let go a spurt,
                          a little thin skin cracked and loosened,

propelled yourself up the hill and into the ladies & gents and
cookies tasting of wallpaper paste . . . your ideal in her perfect suit
went by and glad you'd sewn the button on at the last.

You are alone but don't listen.

All of literature rains down lots of commas.

And even feel fine most evenings, sliding into the flowered sheets so
relieved to have your spreading to all corners two could fit in easily.

Bones fall gently towards the floor, you sleep with
regular breathing.

It's the unexplained wakings and where they leave you.

In a clearing
with someone who loved you
alive in the dark.

You are brave. But you need to be touched.

THE FAULT

too much energy she tried to show with
her hands moving outward

how it smothered
how one's joy could create fear like yeast in the shy person

I was circling this, sniffing
what I hadn't paid attention to other times

that his hairs were all yellow gold
wiring out of a center of energy &

I felt myself in love with him watching his tongue run over his lips
and remembered Fredericka

                  always keeping the tube of vaseline in her purse
always gliding it over her mouth should there be someone to kiss

and thought how I liked space and long unending lines, how my life
was that way, without visible connections or obvious explanations

                            how I was glad

I'd washed my hair

HIT-AND-RUN

Dear Eric, the moon is

FULL

and hot white and hung simply in the black sky.

I would like to turn off the light to write you this message but
the typewriter letters are black and would not shine
as the moon does,
                        and when the moon's shine hits the panes of glass
on my back porch windows, its light reveals

an energy in the glass (a way in which it was polished, maybe?)
that whirls with that very centrifugal motion Van Gogh always tried
to get down in his starry night paintings.

Well, he was a man. Ecstatic. Suffering. Like you.

My hands are cold, the wind leaks in between the cracks of old wood
holding the windows together. You will always be someone I can talk to.
And the moon's being full
                        reminds me it's exactly a month since we were
walking in slow motion out the door of the Roosevelt Tamale Parlor,
heading for a good movie,
                        when that drunk came tearing around the corner
and headed straight for the trunk of my Datsun.
                        All the boys in the Mission
ran up shouting about the big white pick-up truck with red lights strung
across its back, and a formal insurance man in a brown suit
handed me his card.
                        I can write you this way because of Frank O'Hara,

because everything was important to him, even hit-and-run drivers
and unfinished evenings, which ours was, how we barely got through
the hard part, to get to what comes after that,
                                    the difference
one doesn't really notice, but takes in like milk.

COINCIDENTAL

Half of my friends accuse me of excess
(waiting on line and trusting in inches)
The other half lean
and have given up glossy fenders with their little pockmarks of rust

It is comforting to know that these same accusations
keep company among the ducks fighting for bread from your fingers
using their beaks with concentrated fury

Revulsion has been mainly a failure
and so has dabbling,
                              while exactness can rest
in one hand, smoothly
as a fertilized egg
                              Without knowing, one might be listening
for the crack which would merely indicate a vulnerability,
the delicate parabolic strength in the egg's curve
beyond our power to reduce it

"Physics" becomes more cheerful each day and delights
in breaking the "laws of nature"

While quantums flow backwards, our children on skate boards
are pulled up into the sky
in the same way that Christ was swallowed by white clouds

One might call this a sort of rapprochement—the unthinkable light

You must elaborate or ascend   One chooses to pay attention

to the movement, an output of plant roots or
the possible expansion under each arm
where the breath might flow freely   and in dignity

We feel how all the little clutches of the body seem finalized
as though some law of physics told us to hold ourselves tightly
and not let any part fall out
                    any messy tear
or a tearing-out of the red female parts inside last night's dream
where I often visit the passage to see how far things have moved

Rigorous methods have been established to capture the elusive,
a fanatic devotion to statistics and controls,
                    but
we secretly pray to ghosts as they hover among the teeth of gears
We feel our muscle systems quivering, as though trying to get loose

A great urge to be down-to-earth seems to show up in each generation
You can slice it as you would a flatworm for a microscopic study
or shuffle it or randomly select
well-bathed individuals and place them in an antiseptic
atmosphere
and still the tiny jiggles of light persist,
as though some boogaloo of joy insisted on having its way—
a full tank, a sunny day, a mailbox stuffed with envelopes

NEW SHOES

(or why I cross out words)

You know
those shoes
you bought, with
the platforms
and shiny leather
insteps
and holes cut out,
which I admired
so, well
you bought them,
not because it was
snowing
but probably
because there was
some hole
or rundown heel
on your other pair
and you didn't want
it to show,
or else
you got bored

with your good old
shoes,
so well-constructed
and always
there
to take you

where you needed
to go
but one day you
looked out
the window
and you wanted
to take off
to a place
you couldn't think of
where those shoes
wouldn't do
wouldn't dance
enough and
lift you into
the new
arrangement

well, that's why
I cross out words
so thoroughly,
as though I never
said them,
when I did,
and felt I did,
and knew what I'd said,
and felt it
to be
so well-constructed
that it would
keep saying
itself
that way,
automatically moving
ahead,
when I
no longer wanted to.

Part II

Without Voice, What She Witnessed

FLOWERS

Changing water. Adding aspirin. Nitrogen, potash or
sugar (white) to keep limpness from descending
upon these purple and magenta asters with broad golden centers
and petals packed in two rows making fringe above
green spread leaves, still alive. Keep cutting stems
to retain the vertical pull of water up into
the barely charged life.

She said there was a tiny charge of energy *still*, like a cord moving
between me and the child—a girl—though its body life had stopped
after four months, only one leg intact on the fetus. "It's better," the
doctor said. "Nature knows best," he said, at the end.

That was ten years ago. He was pulling me along on an immaculate
silver table, larger than a serving tray, I thought, sheet over me
then, white linen, and their faces soothing. Shapes of words and
eyes. I couldn't identify. Something inside me had broken, though I
tried to hold it in. Red, on everything.

In the white stone pitcher I always place flowers.
First water, then the spiked metal frog
where each flower is stuck in arrangements of
height, darkness or intensity of bloom. The accidents
interest me. The Japanese effect of less.
Space showing its wandering shape between leaves
and the sudden curve of a stem
dying slowly towards what light is
in the room. One forgets about hunger,
absorbed in the fuchsia and the mauve.

SOMETHING KEEPS GLISTENING

Something keeps glistening,
something keeps wanting to move
her eye
beyond that room, where
the child sleeps
under fuchsia darkness woven.

It is the round moon, she thinks,
whose shape tilts dangerously
into completeness.
It shows her
the temptation of solidity,
a marble, dark orange,
rolling
so soon behind clouds.

It is the child's bell, she thinks,
pulling her
in breezes, to the open window,
with its golden paper tongue
dallying.

And what have we really said
to one another, she thinks

again, again.

And what might that silence be?

IN THE DARK, A CHAMELEON

In the dark a chameleon waits
in its green skin   body stretched along leaf
or bit of tree branch   broken off
and fit into glass terrarium with
potted palm fern and narrow electric lamp
running the length of the glass roof
to simulate light and heat   as if
from moist desert shallows

His tiny ribs expand and contract
His scarlet dewlap blows up
for mosquitoes   or the female of his species
Elbows and knee joints are delicately scaled
and placed at exact angles
seizing first   in his mind
the flying thing that will feed him

David watches at a distance
but the animal knows
through its little ear hole
who is near and breathing   They share
an infinite patience   in the dark
each slowing down his breath
and body   to track prey
David imagines himself as a force
Then he dreams himself in a moist glass room
with an eye (the size of a reptile's body)
peering in at him   sometimes blinking

From leaf to branch
the chameleon shifts   cell by cell
from green to gray-brown   barely visible
Only his eyes are bright
as though a leaf had fallen
sticking to each lid   even when
the entire mind turns over
trying to protect itself

WITHOUT VOICE,
WHAT SHE WITNESSED

when I could finally climb out and knew I was in my body
on the bed in my usual position it was then
that I felt the other body behind me

he was lying muscle to muscle exactly and in his strength he was
trying to crush me his shoulders sinewy as in medical textbooks his
arms wrapped closer and closer about me so I was pushing trying to
get free of his legs the shock of no face on him I wanted to breathe,
I was biting his thumb in the first direct contact

meanwhile, our routine: David running barefoot to his morning pee
poached egg for your protein   water tap leaking cold trickle

NOTES TO LYN, SHIMMIN RIDGE,
TWO YEARS LATER

This morning I felt a darkness begin to shift
and made myself available, locking the door

I brushed my hair and pulled it back behind my ears
with a silver clasp
                    so as to have no single hair caress
                    or distract my attention;
then I washed my skin clean
and rubbed oil into the hurt places, trying to protect myself

I pulled on the soft old thermal undershirt Dick bought for me
five years ago in Vermont, and some wine-colored tights,
for I felt on my legs the cold of a wind that had come early

in from the ocean, moving, now, against the eucalyptus trunks,
leaning them east and catching in their loose bark
the last hours of light

I knew I could wait no longer, but did not know
what might enter my solitude

I was unhappy with thickness, a kind of withholding
all around me, invisible, but breathing with familiar regularity

I could hear my neighbors walking up and down their steps
carrying brown paper bags full of food
I watched from behind the shades   When a friend came to my door
I sat listening to her knuckle against wood
She needed to kill time

I needed to be perfectly still

.   .   .

In the bay window, now, for hours,
I pull the Guatemalan blanket about my legs
and take in the energy of its color—stripes of melon, acid green
and three shades of blue found in mountain lakes
at different soundings

I think of the weaver in Mitla, who hung her loom from the tree;
I let her stitches take me in and out of their little loops,
their pink doorways

I do not look for anything ahead of time

.   .   .

All day, this pressing, a thirst that won't let me be

I try to begin what I've been putting off
I make a list   I write a difficult letter
Entering the world this way, the light feels garish

(eyes not wanting to accommodate)

Lyn, I feel time pushing, always, from the other side
I want to push back   but the gesture gets confused
What am I choosing?

I am a beginner

Sometimes I catch myself weeping in the street as I am driving along

2

I had made a note to myself, two years ago, to read the contents
of the manila envelope you gave me   I have carried it
like a last bite, the ration of a survivor,

When I think of you, I remember us sitting on the slope

below Shimmin Ridge, not far from the horses   There is sky,
a magnificent blue, protecting us, and a tiny river, below, of silver

shifting the proportion, our place in it   On-going stillness

Your life seemed so complete then, in the meadow, loving, as you did,
Larry, so visibly on you, keeping your face tender

That was the second summer of my grief   body still numb
from disconnection   I could hardly bear to be around such aliveness

I had to keep my eyes half closed

That's how it happened the horse stepped on my foot, later,
leading it to pasture, with David just seven, trying to balance
on its bare back   both, smelling my fear

3

I did not want to love hard   again
I did not want to open myself
I tried to be invisible, eyes down,
a certain skein of busyness

But seeing your face, bony and truthful,
I knew I was mistaken

· · ·

I've just opened
the manila envelope, finally ready to take in
what kept eluding me,

". . . the locus of one's sense of the personal, wherein lies one's
rootedness, and from which one improvises a reality"

The garden's gone wild   Garlic flowers break white
antennae out of long green pods   Yesterday, I began again,
with the weeds, discovering under them
new growths of lemon thyme and purple chive blossom
Dandelions glittery in the grass

David says "Do you think they are pretty?"

He waits for my answer   measures it   I feel myself fight against
what I've been taught to think

"Yes, darling, they are so yellow!"

4 A.M.

In the dream I had my legs around you.
I was someone else.

"I love you," I said.
You couldn't hear me.

You seemed to resemble a man who felt familiar,
warm in bed, smelling good.

You acted your part as you had in other movies.
I was a character too. I said

"I love you. I really do.
Does that bother you?"

You turned your head sideways, looking worried.
You said, "I don't know."

Then a cry broke my sleep; again and again
it came narrowly through the window,

a woman's voice begging for help,
running in the dark. It woke me up.

I ran to the door, straining to locate her terror.
I called your name.

You were standing next to me naked
in the cold air, both of us helpless.

A car door slammed. At that very moment
I felt the scream enter my body, changing me finally.

SPECIAL HANDLING

The light is four o'clock light
though it's only three   & Mediterranean
      Soon   shadows of someone's back steps
      have solidified   and take on depth
            like a door you might
                  want to enter   or
how a black dog's shadow rubs
                              the side
                                    of the
                                          house and
goes down into that same light with little hammer sounds

            On a simulated roof
                  footsteps   drag against green diagonals
                              & beige
                  asbestos siding (fire-proof)
                        because everyone worries about fire
                              sometimes
            how flame lights up the body   licks holes

Inside the house   she takes baths
            to make the fire go away
      The water holds   has its own   open arms
            a wet bridge under her
                  carrying her forward   away from mud
      She tries for similar effects in blue pools
            though bodies do bump up
                  against her
in the reverie of a smoothly executed

                lap in which no
                        error appears in the stroke

        But in a tub   above Pacific waters   you just float
                going nowhere
                        a boat moored inside a hill
                                with the moon stuck
                alee   & spilt wherever
                                hair's free

        Entering
        the underground water   it will be warm
                with minerals that tattoo   their shadows beneath
                the silver rings on your fingers
                        But don't worry   go in
                        by the back road   and know any mud
                                is just darkness getting thick
                                        not dirty

        The risk is
                        in stillness   to rub up against
        that special handling light gives us

"THE KNOW"

For Laura Wessner

Not overwhelming, this morning's little dream
      hot white squares
            of sun soaking through
                  opaque tattered shades, then
window   wind   oh window light falls in
            on a vision of future neat stacks:
                papers letters announcements falling,
      now filed under   "mouth" or "flower"

Just pressing them together   pushing them flat
with glass paperweight
         depicting beige cliffs and
            half a curved bridge   diagonal trestles
               vertical in white puffy clouds
                  and the intimate blur of somebody's house
        under trees   at the edge of a thought
            called "paradise"

            All that
               calls for absolute attention
     at each moment   separate
        Being in the now is not
what they called "the know"   or is it   I am
          solidifying into a constant flow
            roots going down sideways for water
       In sleep fragments,
         I jogged with D. in pasture   passed long slabs

of old wood   brownish grey from smoothing of water
        our thought   between us running

    as this attempt to reach you, Laura,
            through air
Still shots, of purple under your eyes   spread of blood vessels
            rooted   like some new Japanese eye-shadow
    where they   broke your nose   on the inside   to let you
            breathe
                The bruises made me think "pain"
            when you walked in   that someone had hit you
        but it was just you   coming through time
                and trying to evolve into the air
            borne species you sense
                in those wingtips at your heels
                    you imagine for someone else   .   .   .

        .   .   .   your "cowboy," I think
    You give him your best shots, always
        and in between   tender
            towards his "testicles like petals"
                the pink soft wrinkled edge of both
        your warm shores
                There is more, I wish I knew where
    the corner is   to turn   Still poised
        in this light, feeling all digital glow
                this message is a conviction
        from someone sprung into the joy of not knowing

FLOOD

Dear someone, sometime
    in a panic
  in your mind
     you hide behind
my hot indifference
    which you imagine warily
  to be conceptually strong
     as celluloid intelligence.
But over here, where it's dark out,
    I'm just me
      feeling uneasy in these nights
cold and black.
       I turn the heat up
    higher
     thinking other people's lives
are warmer,
    suffer the suspicion
       I'm mediocre,
   remembering how
Gauguin whispered
   Be Mysterious.
Into wood he cut it

Soyez Mysterieuses

above the backside of
a female body
lying perfectly
voluptuous
in mud
or sleeping (was it?)
as if pillowed
and dreamy with her legs
explicitly
not there
but held in darkness
under wild waves curling
where his tool entered
wood
showing us
his choice for her
impacted
in the prolonged watery beat
always sleeping
face sideways
with flesh of body
soft   white   wanting
to nod out
of what the next cut
might reveal.
The message moves forward
like a Ouija board
with its own hands
Soyez Mystérieuses.
You get the joke.
Babyhood becomes us
and is still yours
for one night. I offer it
as evidence

and then it's my turn;
	now you be the strong one,
Lady mama, Queen somebody.
	Aslant,
		you appear
			in relief
	but feel yourself
		moving out of the old
			female sleep.
You hear the intellect
	of cells
		turning over,
	recognize
		in another's gaze
a different subject, not merely
	"you" and "me" not even
	representational or
		seductive
			but hungry for breakfast
	under waking Pacific sky
		and eager to swim out.
			I want
				to turn this body
	over,
show you her face
		awake and askew,
	imperfectly ready
		to re-write
			the flood,
		nothing in the way,
			all of the body
					seen
		in motion.

Part III

The Story of Emma Slide
(as found in her Accounts Ledger)

NOTES ON EMMA SLIDE

In December of 1973, a name fell into my mind. The name was Emma Slide. I'd never known anyone by the name of Emma. Nor had I been consciously asking a question, to which this might propose an answer. But I liked the name immediately and it began to take on some charge. Soon it was a she. I was in the dimestore buying an address book, and spied a small ledger, black bound in red leather with gold lettering. I bought it with no purpose other than my sensual delight in its proportions and colors. When I got home, I suddenly thought of my new friend Emma. I wrote "The Story of Emma Slide" in the front of the ledger and in the next few days conceived of a long poem, composed of journal entries made by this persona. It would be an investigation of romantic love, as it was breaking down in the life of a baffled, confused woman whose need for intimate love had pushed her into a relationship lit by clichéd expectations. Then the lights went out. And there were two people.

Emma Slide

I'm a sly ddd e

in the long voluptuous metallic
stroke/   of the Electrolux   I went down

stroking the unconscious   as in water

the beak-to-wing-tip glide of

      the free fall

          ing body
          through light

"a tunnel that never ended" David called it

discovering how she who thought
she was this shape of Emma
with points of reference
this warmer of plates

      but just below the skin
        was so small
        so small
        she was
      all in a pool
    in an overflowing of help me

Entry, 12/31/73

Emma's confused. The water's too much. It comes down in
tiny perfect seeds all the day long. She can't get through
it. Can't make headway. Headlong. Long gone Emma. Gone
with the wind. Out the window, her arms and legs go,

    as a starfish in the very center of the "world" is
    pointing five directions at once/all the symmetry
    of it pulling against its off-center center.

Here she is, facing "everything she ever wanted" and still,
those firm wishes just wash away on leaky days.

You look around for little duties—they are measuring cups
and provide you with accomplishments you can offer to a
friend. You say "Have a cookie," though she or he may
be just a picture of someone you talk to in your imagination.

Today there is a man in Emma's life.
He is every good thing, almost.
But nothing works.
Can it be possible that this vibrational field of deep touch
leaves her yet with her self?
Oh dissatisfactions of brain life. Is it the left side or the
    right?
Whatever.
It breaks.

What was it the water said? Lay back. She tried to listen,
to line her body up with the rainy creased flow.

So nice. His kindness. His hands pulling her in.

Wandering into the kitchen. Coffee to heat. Not being able
to focus while someone's *there*.

In the space: lemons, coleus plants, the seven-year-old boy
and sometimes his friend.

She needs a door.
Emma needs a sliding door to open and shut, to be herself
behind, without thinking.

His body in hers, her body keeps remembering. All day.
The many days. Now moments where the body rides warm and
radiantly solar at the base of the spine and all inside her.
The tunnel of heat. How his hands again open her to it,
against all skepticism, all hurt.

She goes down in herself. Says bye-bye to the world on the other
side of her skin.

It's green. It's a plant. Touching its grape-like leafy stretch,
she notices how it makes itself out of its center—fresh stems
leaning up and the tiny beginnings of a shape.

Is this what she wants? A repetitive nature.
No, but to grow plant-like and tendrilly
from the center
but new.
The shapes with their important differences
                    and the translucent veiny journeys.

Entry, 1/3/74

Ledger   on the ledge   an accounting of here I am again with my
nose against the glass

Emma visits the perfect rooms of another, the house pushed out
above the water on pilings   long struts of wood   glass walls
the only separation between

               her body

               and the skids of gray green bay water

a white healthy gull

white health

Always having to face each other

Bach harpsichord music rolling along tin wires

(wanting to do something private, secret, alone   Unknown to the
other   To be free of the *self*-consciousness that the other's pres-
ence brings in,
               habits I don't want to know about)

This sky takes its color from the sea   so much of it surrounds us

Bound up or feathered with its softness   gray pillowings
and softer for the dark green edge of the hill

                                        Entry, 1/5/74

turning, two hands, a full circle
one more hour dropped in the day/a duck diving

                  below the satin water light
                  and never surfacing

Inside, behind glass, Emma watches, snug

The man, her little cup of fantasy, he's up the stairs
and in bed watching the sky slide right past the windows.

"Look," he says. "Look up."

Through the sky-light something moving, shifting.
Birds make black wing prints. Slide and change. The inches
between them

             poised at the crisp edge of order.

What was the difference? Loving someone, or

               being "in" love . . .

She suddenly didn't want to share.
She didn't want to hear his asking for a bit of everything she was
tasting. His finger in her marmalade. His ears alert to the
sound of her tooth crunching.

                                  Entry, 1/6/74

(Emma meets the moon)

The moon that day should have made it perfect

        A love affair perfectly shy and full

        in its round light

In the late afternoon, we climbed the hill
to get more of the moon in us

        it hung there, in overlays of mauve
        blue pink   to make us go oooh

        and drink and drink to fill this big space
        we knew in ourselves
        and could not fill for the other

Perhaps the moon?

        (one always hopes for a mystery to change things)

In bed that midnight we could see it as intense and confusing as a
street lamp, but it was higher

"He thought to bring some of it into the room/it would make me
love him"

But Emma loved the moon
her body opened to it

        and each stroke she felt was the moon's power
                borrowing his fingers

"I knew I did not love him
I knew it was the moon I felt shy before"

without speech   coming   coming closer

Entry, 1/11/74

Down the slide, Emma.

Where are you going?

> "To a place. I want to find a place.
> Always the others seem firm
> and I must seem to them.
> > But someone to love
> as the tendrils of plants want a wall to climb."

Oh, Emma, you are lonely   a body impatient for pleasure

"I thought I knew the place was in me
But it's a gray sea   very wide
Not able to slide through it   to the blue."

Entry, 1/12/74

Emma says ohm   ohm   ohma   oh my

oh my pie in the sky

Emma girl, you've blown it!

All those clouds
the meringue you could have licked from his blue lips

Looking back I see I wanted him
to be   my final solution

I wanted him to pay my dues
take me on a cruise
and never lose sight of me

That way   I wouldn't have to keep watching
out   for Emma

and could slide right out my window

Entry, 2/10/74

Emma sees into herself like a jar. There's a disappointment in
there.
    A him that is a shadow of something that will not overwhelm
her. He's not a phenomenon to be in awe of,
          not to be prayed to on her slant board,
          not to have an emotion named after him, all his own, in
          his honor.
He will not bring the focus of an ending
or the expectation of a gun about to shoot
                 (all lovely adrenalin rushing around
                                  in her).
She wanted him to be the great spectacle. Something to bring her
to the edge.
She wanted to forget everything that hurt and call it little.
She wanted to let go of the tiny hopes that crowded her
          like a shelf where everyone left their safety pins and
          newspaper clippings and never came back for them.
She wanted to breathe out, indefinitely.
To change forms. To unload the gauzy gray stuff mushing the roofs.
Too much she felt a shutting down of the bright flash making the
windows what she needed.

Emma felt in her heart there could mean a beginning.
It was so.
Emma knew.
The light so very light.
But the change refused to come from him. From out there.

Here was the blue kitchen and here was the teapot.
Here was her white hand around the cup.

Late afternoon, the air is small town air, as in November
just before heavy snow.

And he is merely a shine, a part of what is changing.

Entry, 2/14/74

Part IV

Magritte Series

"Even in the realm of the half-conscious, his urge was toward control, consciousness, exactitude. Like Ouspensky, he was familiar with those delicate, brittle states of lucidity during sleep in which the sleeper is conscious of himself."

"This evolution in Magritte's work of pre-Renaissance space, in which movement is frustrated and the depth uncertain, opens up to him the possibility of inventive play with imaginary spaces."

A. M. Hammacher, *Magritte*

LA VIE SECRETE IV /
THE SECRET LIFE

Suddenly there were bruises
at various places
along his left thigh
and just below the knee-cap
he could see the freckles
holding their bits of brown
as the purple flesh
turned to yellow,
but mostly he knew
when the bruised parts of him
came into contact
with other firm objects
and a light but definite
sense of pain
surprised him
and he stopped to
locate it,
to understand the source
and recapture some set of moments
in which his flesh
had received blows
distinct enough
in precisely those spots
he understood now
as tender.
All his body was tender.
But most of it did not know.

L'ASSASSIN MENACE /
THE ASSASSIN MENACES

For M. P.

She noticed how
he used blue
and green
to bring his life
into focus or
sometimes red,
never a simple crayon box red
but a tinge of the bizarre to it,
a leaning towards blue
which would be plum
or suggestive of certain wines
after the war
or even blood, just freshly there
so that the air took its effect.
She knew if
she went to visit him—
if she were invited, or
if she crawled through the window
as he was going
out the door—
that blue
would be seeping from beneath
the pillow in the bedroom.
She could not be sure
about the bathtub.

This made-up quality of his life
intrigued her.
She felt it to be impersonal
in the way that she'd tended
to identify certain male traits
in other men
and yet even
in the basket
where his discarded socks lay
with their vaguely uncomfortable
holes
she noticed a green sock
beginning to unravel
and under it,
spreading imperceptibly,
the red.

LA BAIGNEUSE DU CLAIR
AU SOMBRE / BATHER BETWEEN
LIGHT AND DARKNESS

I am floating,
like being in a tub of water
moving toward the lights.

He is floating in the water,
he is wiping the table
with a dirty napkin.

The place is big.
I can feel it breathing.
We are moving toward the lights.

The dream about my death
drops into my head,
foamy red and almost boiling.

I don't want it to happen
if it's going to hurt.
The things I hear

are going out my left ear
and moving
toward the lights

like a woman wearing a red sweater.
Wearing a red sweater,
I am attracted

by the view behind her,
out the window
at the civilized periphery.

It is clean.
It is highly finished
like these clothes of mine

moving toward the lights.
I'm sliding down the bench
into the scenery

out the window
towards the woman.
I'm thinking about inertia

as the wall vanishes.
The woman is dancing.
I am thinking about the woman

sliding toward the lights.
The red sweater vanishes.
Again, the ending gets a little vague,

as she slowly puts her arm
around his shoulder, as she slowly
puts a dagger through the bones

in his chest. She puts lights
in his chest. Her arm is
a big cloak. Pieces of him glow

all over the room.
I recognize nothing
but the color of brown

wrapping paper. Now
she's giving me
the big present.

L'INVENTION COLLECTIVE /
COLLECTIVE INVENTION

of the marigolds, of blue vinyl suitcase, of crud all over the stove
she'd left shiniest
    two to bring light to,
    yes a shelf in reach where the little both of them could begin
    could make his clean start as fresh as Watermelon slice (oh
    where was her life?)
        in him his tiny mysteries her laughing sound alight
        in his throat

        oh what was a mother to do, being her, and suddenly
        it's now?

when she went away there was this big boy who pushed him
when she went away they pushed him in the puddle
he was running home, he was running home and she wasn't there

but trying somewhere else to find out who
and where, was she?

        was she not the neat and tidy? did she not see
        her seducers in a line and shaking their fingers and showing
        "be here, be here"

in her mind (was it?) she lay at the edge of the waters, at the
edge of the waters
    was it sand there? was her fish skin bare? all she knows is
    it scratches and when the waves collapse in inches she cannot
    swim for her finny body's half human.   One day she's
    plunk on the shore and her image comes to her   in a picture
    as though holding a mirror of blue paint

just a whiff of horizon and the little waves creeping
and folding   and there it is, no way of turning her
back now   her thighs/knees, softest whirring of
crotch hair   and all the color of how she ought to be
but suddenly those fins
and the beginning of silver slippery fish-lady lying,
no arms no woman swimming, but a face cut deep with
gills and the sad eyes panting

and the absolute quiet of something about to arrive.

LES VALEURS PERSONNELLES /
PERSONAL VALUES

As a child she'd often considered the bathroom as her future, how it would be if it were her place to be alone in. Under the porcelain sink would be the stove. Next to the toilet, the radio (there was just enough space). She could sleep in the tub. Under it her blanket would be folded. There would be apples. A flashlight. Her mystery books. And no one would come in there. No one would be asking her to be good. All the mess would go away.

Later she chose a boat. It appeared to her in a dream, before rising, and was smoothly crafted in the shape of a canoe but made of many pieces of wood of a natural nut-brown color. Its insides were sleek. She could manage, feeling the lift of the water under her. There was her comb leaning against one side, and a little mirror hung just under the seat. It would send out light, little flashes of it, to make it seem as though there were an electric storm about to approach. But caught in one corner, to maintain the sense of home, a curtain of soft white cotton, as though a window were behind it, to open, if one wanted, or to look out of. For surely, white clouds caught in the precise boundaries of the window's rectangle would give one a different sense of motion, of how long it took a cloud to float from one edge to the other. On the floor of the boat, she imagined an oriental rug, opulent but of a proportion not to overwhelm the purity of the boat's intention. It fell into character, providing backdrop. Often she would place several objects there—a wooden match with yellow sulphur tip or one of those rich cakes of soap with beveled edge, oval, smelling of apricot, never touched, yet reflected in the mirror in two parts, as if used or broken.

This morning she'd awakened smelling the sea. Before thought, she'd noticed an urgency in her left foot to dangle in the water, and it crept up into her body, pulling, wanting the openness of the sea, the wetness, wanting her body to be taken into the largeness without any walls, no object to distract her into order. She felt the boat tipping. She felt the possibility of doing nothing to stop it.

LES JOURS GIGANTESQUES /
THE TITANIC DAYS

Have you noticed the little shadow?
  How when you are in the middle of brushing your teeth
  there is something gathering around the corner?
She is dreaming this thought to a self
awake in the world
when she feels a tug, something like a hand pressing
down upon her thigh
  and she remembers she is naked and alone in the room
  and wishes for her silk blouse
  and the zipper with its three silver hooks at the top.
In her body's emptiness
a growing sense of intimacy,
the pressure of a shadow in its black suit,
its right hand moving
around her waist, as if looking
for a pocket,
  or the push of a head against
  her shoulder, as though
  this movie from some little light booth
  on the opposite wall was focusing,
  on her, and the image was him,
  his half head
moving towards her nipple,
with the thirst in him, black
against her white body. She looks down,
  she looks down at, oh, the hand, or is it
  the shadow of a hand
  pressing in on the thigh that is hers.

Her muscles bulge with effort
and become tremendous
in their flex. The color drains
from every part of her, but
    the red mouth,
        holding its shape steadily,
        the scream, at first uncertain,
        enters the air
        and becomes the third,
        the knowing, between them.

LA REPRODUCTION INTERDITE /
NOT TO BE REPRODUCED

For Dick

I am interested in the logic of secrets, how it has always moved me, in particular, to be invited by a face into the aura of its withholding, as though we were designed to bring forward two opposing sets of facts and bathe ourselves in the resulting struggle, as in watching a tightrope walker move from one point in space to another, each foot brought precisely from behind and placed in front of the other, but without the delicious possibility of falling, were it not for the rope stretched tautly beneath him, cutting the air with its odor of hemp.

The secrets between men and women are of peculiar fascination. My father, for example, invited me into a dream last summer where I discovered that he was making preparations to die. He was busy doing small errands, rushing about in his impeccably tailored suit and polished shoes, with a face so sad, so preoccupied with its secret, so designed to escape observation that I immediately began to pay attention, invited as I was by that closed-off expression to become the rope upon which he demonstrated his journey.

As I watched him moving to get everything in order before leaving, my sense of dismay began to take on its own life, expanding into anger and then curiosity. "How does he know?" I asked my mother. The fibers in me were twisting and vibrating. A conviction was growing. I became filled with the possibility of his life continuing and decided to speak to him directly, hoping to convince him that his death need not be imminent.

I go to my father and I say "Why do you think you are going to die?" His feeling is more one of resignation or tiredness than any specific illness. I ask him matter-of-factly to take off his clothes so that I may look at his body. He does so and his body appears to be fine, a bit shorter and stockier than I remember, but ruddy and glowing. I see immediately that he is perfectly well and able to live for a very long time. I tell him with conviction and energy that there is no reason for him to continue on this course of dying, that he is wholly alive and has many things to do. As I tell him this, we are walking outside through a woods, now up a slight incline to a clearing. My father seems very joyous and happy to hear the news. He accepts it, but with a kind of privacy that he's always had, savoring it for himself, indicating that he hopes I won't make a public issue of it. There is a kind of charged excitement between us, a flirtation with the possibilities that now lie ahead.

In 1965, my father was hit by a car and pronounced dead. I asked for his first set of architect's drawing tools, wrapped in a chamois case he'd sewn himself, each metal pencil and compass enclosed in its own soft pocket, each a potential source of precision and invention, given a hand to hold it.

L'ELOGE DE LA DIALECTIQUE /
IN PRAISE OF DIALECTIC

On the plumped-up couch (it was scratchy wool stuff
of couches made in the '30's), their thighs rubbed,
diverging in similar directions,
parallel but inaccurately compared to anything else,

                and soon
the vision of that summer, unexplained by logic
but still new and rolling into view,

              was there in the room.
At least she thought she felt
something shifting, a quality you couldn't measure but feel,
and it was autumn. In California, bright orange pumpkins
popped up in various sizes and flung themselves over the fields
near the ocean, a broad merging of blues and grays.

              But here,
mist hung around the house like a mood
and what had been playful and sexual in the summer
seemed to verge on melodrama by its very withholding
and the possibility of someone important arriving at any moment
through the gauze curtains,
reducing the sharpness of the light even further.

She had come with her suitcase and a certain equilibrium
not available at an earlier time.
There was business in the world
and there was memory. Wounded on army cots holding hands.

              How did they
get their clothes off? Had the light been on? Was that really
Tito Puente's mambo coming through the heating unit under the desk?

The age of bitterness had receded. A relief. That useless system
of blame, of someone else or of the self, even worse
a circle as predictable as the gold circle pin they used to wear
in the East, to show good taste.
                              He was tasty. Of that she was certain.
His blond beard, which she'd often remembered as black,
was something she liked to pull on, hard. Or just sift her fingers
through it, thinking of clouds, of a Georgia O'Keeffe
bluescape with
                    puff   puff   puff   of various whites
unattached to
any set of values but the last stroke, when the painter stopped
for a moment of thought, as the phone rang or the coffee boiled
over, and never came back.

But she came back,
not expecting anything but touch. Was it in the hot room
or next to the lake? There was a path, too, that made the journey
to supper longer and it was there, she thought, their minds touched
without plan.
                    How does one recognize these certainties?
                    To think of kissing, behind dialectic.

Their sentences climbed together, if there had been stairs,
but everything was flat, it was summer and spacious on the outside,
though the corridors always had bodies in them and the urgency
towards motion, predicting a scene already played out.
She was not interested in that,
though she seemed to walk at the same speed as the others. So
when he kissed her, as common as kisses are, it was not common
because she hadn't arranged it in her mind.
                              And here they were, now,
on the rosy couch, with winter hovering, about to break in through
the gray air and their hour was almost up. They had kissed again
and wanted more

but even that wanting could not expand because
the window was planned to reveal life in a little town
at any moment. Someone could walk by. Someone could look in. And
oh, his life was happy.

LA REVOLUTION /
THE REVOLUTION

For A.

Everything is so agreeable, tangential, so light
of foot.
        Tangerine, all pungent with its leaves intact.

Still, revolution is your quietest intent,
it throbs through your kindness like a double bass
without amplification,

but you are persistent and grow a callus of light
from so often stroking the gut strings.
                      You hold

its body next to yours, in the air,
and when you play in the key of C
molecules forget their lesser purpose
                     and turn swiftly
          breathing the new physics.

          I listen. You invite me to care on a grand scale.
          What must I leave behind me?

Like you, I give the finger to
standing still. I'm tactile.
Here are all my fingers to place inside yours.

Looked at, loosely, within any frame of reference,
I could seem predictable.
Don't be fooled. Bumpy ovals of color thrill me.
Tangentially.

I count on your intelligence, with or without you
sitting there. Still, I want more.

Perfection begins to hurt because
love feels dangerous
                        and only one of us is you,
only one of us is taking the other's temperature. It might be me.
But that could be over-simplified, since you often choose
not to tell.

What do you notice, awake? I notice I'm afraid to break in on
the fluidity. My dreams ask questions,
                        the ones I've thought about
                        but can't speak.
Sleeping next to you counts for a lot.
Your shadow wrestles with mine. The glow is Kirlian. What you hide
in the revolution pours intimately through the dark.
Its effect can't be measured in the "real" world.

All controls break down. The sheets convey your deepest sigh
to my body. You are not alarmed because we don't say a word.

Part V

Now That the Subjunctive Is Dying

ON THIS DAY AWAKENED

On this day, awakened
early,
by the dog's bark,
she saw the sudden gray lake, rising,
below her window,
mists
she had not been told of,
thickness, unexpected,
massing soft
above the bean stalks,
scratched by raspberry and black-
berry thorn, on the underside,
where she knew
the interior landscape
retained its form.

Entering the bushes
the evening before this,
she'd looked for the ripe,
sweet berries,
how the darker pink wanted
gathering
and when she touched them,
she thought of her own
pink nipples,
how he would look
at them, the palest parts
deepening to dark rose,
depending upon their duration,

under sunlight, how he
would taste
the girl in her
and thicken, then, to
the darker.

LOCATIONS

For Bill Evans, jazz pianist

Light forgetting itself   light falling loosely
deep into May

Trying to listen to all that presses up
from under each side
of the seam

Holes where something gives in
to a pulse   careful stitches unraveling

cross-hatch of insulated wires
black slow curves among the poles
street slopes   here
in shadow where houses
lean on each other

but light still
catching white oil tank   distinct against
blue haze above bay water

Pollution soothes us in early evening
we breathe in and forget
coffee no longer hot   wind coming up
flapping the shades

Red metal pot the color of poppies

His love
the spot on the white tablecloth
after dinner

*   *   *

To give up
finally   to stop holding
the infant idea   how deep
you've been told to hurt,

to dissemble the structure
of wounds which choose
to resemble one another

Someday, because he was an exquisite set
of gestures, you thought
still   you would escape
the yearning to be surprised infinitely

A home inside yourself.

Your body held unto itself.

There were ways of talking.

*   *   *

He plays his piano in big cities
and now you are alone with him

in the full amplification
of ambiguous chords which he trusts
silence to justify

What is waiting for you
to fall into

big saxophone body
pulling from another side
of the seam
of music no longer
automatically
dropping

An effort to leave the window
justifies the question of
which is more important:

to witness
last light of mauve sponge sky

or, an inclination towards sound
drifting through the cities
where you listen
to what he isn't telling you,
clearly ambiguous
and totally intimate

. . .

How she notices, is a formal fact
clearly evident as a chip of paint
knocked off perfect white flow

where someone's brush tried to see a wall

Amplification attempts to make it all
all right

and in times of sorrow
a voice turned up loud
can be a true resonance

Still, some sound was too pretty

an easy beat
where you could get stuck,
not finding out

Two trout bought for supper, to please his mouth,
now softening under their scales
She'd know if their eyes were dead
Lights just went out

Their scales were silver and excited her
in a room she didn't talk about

      • • •

Summer, such a little place

full of fish in rivers leaping   The apples out,
red with yellow streaking their sides,
not so glamorous as stores promised
but pulling low on branches next to the road

All in heaviness
to be crushed into softness   Her sweet throat
Cider drinks   gravel you hear first
from the driveway
before the shadow appears   and then
the visual body of the guest

      • • •

These acts of attention   to fill in
all the gaps
where his body keeps going away

THE RECOGNITION

For A.

Pulling myself up to   surface   shimmer in
the tonality
of how you set a mood   It's so casual
when we sit with our drinks   as if
we were finally grown-ups   your story
told always in context of
Turkish cigarettes
         so white   smooth   clean
as though bravery didn't enter into it
is what
I can't get used to   Want a nail to rip
your shirt   no, not something mean, but
the recognition
that this weather in bright blue focus
is fickle   dangerous   lifting both of us
and could change us   We share
this malleable fact   and air
when polluted and thick gray
forcing cell after cell   to murmur,
close down   When I thought

of seeing you   I was wary
felt warned
noticing the delicate fern
near windowlight   had dried up
from lack of water
suddenly every leaf

backing off from its original intensity
sharp greens muted   to loss of   pigment
(old stain on paper)   I thought
this time I did not want
to be the good scotch   the pink pearl eraser
acquiescent   to your saying
all is well   All is not well
I want to take off my clothes
and lie on cool sheets with you and show you
my fever
I want you to look   at me   and say
you're burning up

THE JOURNEY

For the painter, Roy DeForest

Zig-zaggy particles from the West, her eyes' red energy moving
in a steady vertical of
                    please identify yourself or at least
come half-way,
                    even horizontally,
these uncovered breasts flaunting nipples magenta
and barn red blush of torso flesh   rooted into

that line where the sky stoops in landscape.

But isn't this the sea?

Lying later around, no modesty on deck, a varnish like sun-
light, her vector extends in red sugar dots to its opposite . . .

Who to have dinner with? And what next to wear?
Something simple as a Dingo. Something black as a dog with
every hair in place.

Walking openly on deck, of ship, does anyone object?

This journey, with her breasts to the sea wind. Not entirely nude,
not ideal, but a real person (the 20th century article), savoring
her almost invisibility, so round, so pulsing,
bare feet against deck wood and newness of no one's little hand
to hold.

So green her pleasure, she could wait forever.

Inside her heart, meanwhile, or stomach part, all is revealed
in a picture where she's kissing her philosopher in a canoe
(it's blue)
and for now they can't row far

                        because of the frame.
But near is what she wants and he's here
with the hard-core dangle of a Dingo, and a smile, too,
saying

        We are forever rowing toward each other
        With our hermetic reds and greens. Not to be tame.

DEAR LAURA, IN DECEMBER

Dear Laura, in the pause that has lengthened
      between us   I imagine your face
         as David described it—Mexican
    with Chinese eyes—
              sniffing face powder from Hong Kong
              so white where it fell
  on the rug   among blue flowers   Christmas
      morning   There is always someone
          about to be born   The snow
           falls lightly first
    and peregrine falcon waits
          on a high branch
      Even your boredom has the fragrance
          of alertness
in this white tissue   green smalltown air

Our mother (yours or mine) is the only one
        given us   so
          it is hard to allow
            ragged weather
  under her striped wing and talon
      In the Rauschenberg work you sent, she is
          standing on toes   head tipped back
    as though hunting for something airborne
                  not there yet
        Inky blue fades into femur,
  breasts ballooning like swimsuit ads
and her own very round thighs
          kissing each other's
             tallow and wicklight

What is that darkness? she murmurs
          inside herself   pushing it
          tentatively
                    out   What hope
     she wraps you in lightly
                         as Chinese face powder
She sees you are a rose with its petals folded
          as if in summer   sleeping authentically
          Or she sees behind you
          a shadow   somebody's   out the window
                    falling

I want to remember this season in layers
                    of color   the year I was ten
          and discovered pointillism
                         red blue green gold silver
     spreading slow hot points
                    on the tree
                         because my mother started up in us this urge
     for more

It was cold in San Francisco on the 24th (before
          the clean rains and the five moaning earthquakes)
     I made chili and the phone began
               ringing   Christmas eve on the street
                    and everyone wanting a bite
          Frances on the way to a party
                         dressed up in orange and pink satins
          opening their little lights like poppies
     Mark in gangster pinstripes recited Wallace Stevens
          I love them for how they imagine their lives
                    into being   You were
               sitting with your "vibrant and colorful" mom
                         in the kitchen in Kutztown, Pa.   sipping tea
          whispering inside yourself a constant storm of

who and who or who and me
waiting for some red pillow life
to discover you   refusing anybody's claim but wanting
a stranger to pull you into
car lights   dark streets   snow

I went out to find wood   I could feel how dark it was
and wanted to make a fire for us   My lover had come
a great distance   bringing violets
and a Japanese comforter   silky with falcons,
beige-feathered and gliding above a blue sea
He wanted to comfort me
When he's here, I believe
it's enough

David keeps trying
to feel the insides of things   to open
the morning's wrappings before it's time
Tomorrow he's ten   he can't keep his hands off

AS IN, A MAN
AFTER MY OWN HEART

This pink sky
      evening stroking me somebody's
   big soft breathing

nothing, not here
      with the narrow track of its absence

    like you, not here

That week, the scratches on your body
      were new, not mine
  I don't leave my trail   I go in

     singing   where no one can
  touch you
      I go in five feet more
  my heart balancing
     in air   where all's soft

Under your thought, you're more here

I lied   I didn't want two black stones
      you brought from a beach with someone
   else's scars   They opened
    their windows to me

I got cold   I could see the water rising
   to a dangerous level
      still moored in your hand with touches
  thumbs I didn't belong to

My heart said No   but a hand opened out
    from sleep   to beauty of stone

                  One-to-one means   mouth to heart

I can't find
    how to keep it breathing
        while you move swiftly through

a same pink evening
    shift loves   so each counts
      and doesn't

    but adds up in
      the soft falling air
          l'air du temps   inside

            heart life leaking

GABIONADE

For Lyn Hejinian

cubes of bouillon (chicken)
                         rolled out from green cylinder
container   an accidental motion

like dice being thrown, with intention

surprised in the movement
what it doesn't introduce   of the personal

thus, the mind is cooled (as in temperature)
by an idea   of motion
surprised at its evocation
                of image: smoke
                            table
                            dealer
                            baize
                            green
                            nighttime

                   "never let me go"

             •   •   •

is this what she means by
mask   or might mean

             •   •   •

reading his difficult passages   and receiving
clearly   yet feeling increasingly
clouds inside
                position : juxta position

my "self"
in fluctuations of temperature   I mean,
feeling pulled along by forces not even quite in one's control and

abhorring the impingement (as against one's body)

yet last week, feeling "in control of the situation"
and happy
released into abandonment   swings of pleasure

thus, could write him
peeling off each garment before him

to naked white   with pink highlights spreading

before him

.   .   .

feeling too apparent now
too much said   of who I am, no longer

there, concretely   defining a response
going backwards now   in the sequence

not unfolding   petals

.   .   .

Should I concern myself with the possibility that you might forget?

.   .   .

Someone was sitting on my bed when I came home

his concentration, held again in the fierce angle
of jaw lightly fretted with copper stubble

(remembering him in October, Rembrandt paint rag
wrapped around his hair   to mark sorrow
beer cans   smell of dope in the studio   my feet
held in his hands)

open lines of force, again   between us
feeling the body pull towards   what?
They call them Blood Tides   waiting
for other guests to finish their stories
and go home   and all that time

feeling the pink ranunculas exploding
against the white wall   here in the room with us

where Patricia had placed them   for my birthday
in Chinese straw basket   among sand dollars,
print of Flemish rabbit tapestry and

coiled silver bracelet A. had given me   who was not
here, except as the unvoiced

•   •   •

"I'll be the leaves and
you be the roots," he said,
turning for a drink of water

•   •   •

I am attempting to erase the presence of him
who is not here   I am teaching myself

something I don't want to learn   Against natural
inclination   Knowing intimately, I survive

and live, in appetite   choice

•   •   •

Erasing a word erases its meaning

Believing, finally, in the small acts of revision

Looking up the word *foresuffer*   and finding instead

gabion: a cylinder of wicker filled with earth and stones, formerly
used in building fortifications

94

gabionade: any structure composed of gabions, as a dam sunk in a stream to control the current (see gabion);

. . .

I'm confusing two different stories,
she said; I know I'm mixing them up.

. . .

black space   moon filling out
again

Sutro Tower blinking off-and-on   red   signals

at bedtime, reading to David, it says: "From the earliest times, men have yearned to rise above the earth and fly free through the upper spaces."

. . .

a motion in my mind   without image
called yearning-to-tell-you

BECAUSE YOU AREN'T HERE TO BE WHAT I CAN'T THINK OF

Because you aren't here to be what I can't think of I need most.
Because you aren't pouring me a Scotch with your hands all over the ice cubes.
Because the moon's another streetlight and your lights are off, and on
in someone else's.

Because you warned me thinking you were good but you weren't.
Because I imagine your almost skinny legs and ideal ass from the back
as you put more Debussy on the stereo with the 10 A.M. sun deliciously
licking you.

Because I'm in trouble, hot-headed, bored with the necessary
and can't put on my jogging shoes in spite of their blue Nike stride.
Because your mouth is wistful, off on the grand tour and I want to be
every stop, because you won't stop
long enough to get really scared when you see how deep you go in me,
how deep I come inside you, inside you, let me go
                                                inside you and come up

for more because there are the soft syllabic fruits of Brazil
yet to taste and our twenty juicy fingers' amaroso

on a white cotton shore in what country, is it, meant for us.
Because we are changing

each other's proportions and how much there is
to know, because you still believe you are always in control, oh
a syllogism is a safe place to be but not as mysterious as a rare Chablis.

Because I keep trying to be ambidextrous and adapt to this double vision,
but my eyes hurt and in the last dream you came right in
and went to sleep on my floor.
Because I want to tell you the truth and you think of yourself
as not truthful enough, but you listen, and are sometimes coming nearer.
Because the old stories, you know them backwards, you know them forwards
and they need more pictures in them with windows and doorways and
smoke drawn in pencil curling out the chimney.

Because it's getting late
and you know you can fool almost anyone but me, but so what.
There you are now in your fabulous brown Italian shoes and Egyptian cigarettes,
the man whose soul I love and chest (under cotton shirt) which I bite into
with this thought, in spite of those not quite open eyes
so intent on their hiding you are careful of.
Because there's a saxophone playing between our telephones but you can't
pick it up

because of your other life, the life that came first,

                                        that comes
first tonight, even in our city, life I came after, and other lives
that I continue to come after, because logic always dictates an order,
reasonable, one before two, two before three, because I will not always
be she who is willing to be logical, not always be two, three.
Because I love the new, in you, and the years of us,
                                        but listen closely
when you tell yourself to me, how you never want to hurt again,
someone. As though only one of us were some one.

Because I want to do it, let's do it to a brassy Salsa trumpet,
because I'm not on a dancefloor with you, but here,
hanging out with my shadow over a city of windows,
lit-up, imagining another kind of life almost like this one.

NOW THAT THE
SUBJUNCTIVE IS DYING

The interior pulse of loosely closed mouth after love,
   roof and tongue in that pause of
      not what might be, but learning
each seam of you, how plum and
         undulant life of testicles goes on
        tenderly, soles of feet
   in water, yours, if only candlelight
      piles up on porcelain edge
        of tub to fall off with glide
         of soapy skin.

Now clouds blowing towards us, the dark's away
   in a mid-day light that might have been Italian,
      pigeons, on the other side of glass five floors up
      in wind marked with faint dust streaks,
swoop down, curve in arcs, cut sideways
      given depth by milk-colored stucco
        buildings, shadows in the old style,
summery, and fire ladders climbing down or
     up to antennae. We are lavish
   rooms with many doorways that open out.
         Your face, if that is your body standing
there, suggests the hand on a knob that could be
      possibly
        turning.

• • •

When I left you, those hours, and went for my Saturday massage,
Mary, laying her small brown Sicilian hands on my body, felt the
tightness move off. "Did you feel it go?" she said. "It left. You are so
open today. Something's happening. The door may shut. But he's
opened it. He's standing in it. Listening. To what you might be able
to say. What he can hear."

        ●   ●   ●

touch to tell you   listen, to touch everything

this is   this day, in which someone didn't run away

        ●   ●   ●

Sleep after little sleep, sweet afternoon as if
not disfigured by anyone's time, only bits of fog

hide in air. I lie on your bed reading Rilke and
copying his best lines into my notebook, wake up hours

later, deep in snow drifts, pen still in hand, as though writing.

We were all night finding each others' tongues and knees,
we were all that could have been, in our own finishing.

Still, sleep has taken me into late afternoon with
the corner of your bedspread pulled up over me while

you, on your back, in air, above the couch in the other room,
discover your body below and a girl dreaming of a door.